MAKE YOURSELF PROUD

This journal
    belongs to:

_ _ _ _ _ _ _ _ _ _ _ _ _ _ _ _ _

Make Yourself Proud: An Interactive Life Improvement
Journal by Never Stay Stagnant

Instructions

Don't settle for mediocrity! If you believe, you will. If you need to start somewhere, start here. There is no better time than now. You can do anything you set your mind to.

Okay now that we have the dumb clichés out of the way, let's get this self-improvement party going!

Here at Never Stay Stagnant, we believe in a few rules to life:
1. Never Stay Stagnant...there's a reason it is our name. Keep improving in everything you touch. Continuously change to constantly be a better version of yourself.
2. Be happy. You only have so much time on this planet, so be happy and learn to roll with the punches, knockouts or disruptions.
3. STOP LIVING YOUR LIFE TO SOMEONE ELSE'S STANDARDS. Create your own dream life and go out and reach it.

Sticking to a habit is difficult and starting one is even harder, but we believe you will find joy and ease throughout this journal! There is fun and creativity flowing through the changing weeks. Long gone is the notebook where you fill out the same page 365 days in a row and forget the actual point!

Different tasks you will encounter within this journal are answered with examples in the next couple of pages. It is as simple as a check-in in the morning and one in the evening. Then throw in a Weekly Check-in and you're thriving. If you get stuck on a page, look back here for inspiration or reach out to us. We would love to help you live a Wonderful Life! Quotes are added in for inspiration, but feel free to react or respond to them as you please!

You can use a black pen or have fun with colors. This is your journal, so have fun and be yourself! If you feel like crossing things off instead of coloring, do it! If you want to draw a real-life story in the margins, do it! Whatever you do, just keep up with this journal. Start it on any day that makes sense to you and keep going.

This isn't meant to be a chore, but rather a tool to add tremendous value to your life! We are at the end of your instructions because you should make your own rules in life and you don't need 20 pages to tell you how to be a decent human.

Tag us in your celebration photos, so we can help you celebrate! #makeyourselfproud #neverstaystagnant

Date: _ _ _ _ _ _ _

Meal Prep Day	Meals (breakfast. lunch. dinner)
Monday	Eggs/ Spinach Salad/ Rice and chicken
Tuesday	Eggs/ Spinach Salad/ Veggie Tacos
Thursday	Kale Smoothie with protein/ Chicken
Friday	Eggs/ Rice and Veggies/ Veggie Tacos
Saturday	Pancakes/ Kale Smoothie/ Salmon Salad

The number of hours I slept:

Drink 70oz of water, eat healthy and exercise!

Evening Check-In

How was today great?
1. Ate great food!
2. Finished book about marketing!

Who I look up to:

Sheryl Sandberg

One trait to learn from them:

Confidence

Important things coming up:

- ☐ Moving
- ☐ NSO Project
- ☐ Dinner with girls
- ☐ Rent
- ☐
- ☐

Date: _ _ _ _ _ _

The number of hours I slept:

What steps will I take today to get closer to my goals?

What am I grateful for today?

1. My crazy family
2. People who support my ideas

1. Think about big ideas
2. Marketing Plan
3. Sleep more

Drink 70oz of water, eat healthy and exercise!

How would I rate my eating habits today?

1   2   3   4   5   6   7   8   9   10

Should be dead

Win some, lose some

Put me on the cover of Health magazine

How many ounces of water did I drink?
1 bottle= 8 oz

How many minutes of exercise did I get today?

5   10   15   20   25   30   45   60   REST DAY

Find your joy and let it run your life

My Recipe for happiness:

```
┌ ─ ─ ─ ─ ─ ┐        ┌ ─ ─ ─ ─ ─ ─ ┐        ┌ ─ ─ ─ ─ ─ ┐
│ Sleeping  │   +    │ Doing work  │   =    │ Low stress│
│ enough    │        │ that I love and│     │ and lots of│
│ hours     │        │ am passionate│       │ laughter  │
│           │        │ about       │        │           │
└ ─ ─ ─ ─ ─ ┘        └ ─ ─ ─ ─ ─ ─ ┘        └ ─ ─ ─ ─ ─ ┘
```

Morning Routine
(Cross off all that apply)

What I love
about myself...

My discipline

Drink 70oz of water, eat healthy and exercise!

What I am doing to expand my knowledge

Listening to podcasts and writing down thoughts.

How I ate today:
(draw below)

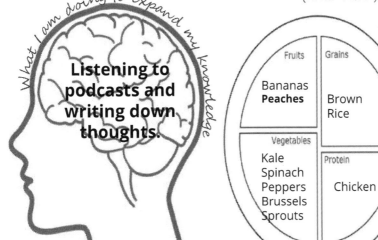

Find your joy and let it run your life

Date: _ _ _ _ _ _ _

How full is my glass?
(positivity in my life)

My friends

Finding my passion

Good people who

support me fully

Description of my perfect partner _____:

- Smart
- Hardworking
- Driven
- Attractive :)
- Gives me space
- Nice but not too nice

Don't settle until I find this!

The number of hours I slept:

Drink 70oz of water, eat healthy and exercise!

Evening Check-In

Don't sweat the small stuff.

What is bugging me?

People judging me with my next career decision

Now let it go!

My comfort zone

Reached out to a mentor!!

Something new I tried out of my comfort zone

Find your joy and let it run your life

Date: _ _ _ _ _ _

Morning Routine
(Cross off all that apply)

What I am learning
from my reading:

Reading a
love story this
week....but also
learned to just
go for it and
ask for
forgiveness
later.

My exercise plan today:

Orangetheory Fitness

What steps I will take today to get closer to **my goals?**

1. Read more business books   2. Sleep more hours   3. Find a mentor

Drink 70oz of water, eat healthy and exercise!

Evening Check-In

How I balanced my life today:

Self-care w/ a mask
Planned night with girls
Hung out with my nieces

Gave full attention to
job
Worked on side hustle

Find your joy and let it run your life

Morning Check-In   Date: _ _ _ _ _ _

What I love
about myself...
My body. It
is my only
one.

My exercise plan today:

Walk 20 min. Weight training.

How I will pay it forward
Buy someone coffee today

The number of hours I slept:

Drink 70oz of water, eat healthy and
exercise!

Evening Check-In

Spend 5 minutes
thinking BIG
(Write or draw your thoughts)

A community that
promotes self-love
through inclusion

What made me happy
today?

⬛ Passion project

🔲 Food

🔲 Working out

🔲 My family

⬜

Find your joy and let it run your life

Date: _ _ _ _ _ _

Issues in my life today:	How I can overcome them:
-sick :(-feeling lost or heading in no direction	-sleep and take more medicine -sit down and think through goals

My Recipe for happiness today:

Eat good, clean food	+	Relax and sleep a lot	=	Rested and fully functioning brain

Drink 70oz of water, eat healthy and exercise!

Evening Check-In

How would I rate my eating habits today?

1   2   3   4   5   6   ⑦   8   9   10

Should be dead   Win some, lose some   Put me on the cover of Health magazine

How many ounces of water did I drink?

1 bottle= 8 oz

How many minutes of exercise did I get today?

5   10   15   20   25   30   45   60   REST DAY

Find your joy and let it run your life

Week of _ _ / _ _

How I spent my time this week:

☒ **Amazing** ☒ **Could be better** ☐ **Bad**

How I did this week:

Productivity		
Healthy Habits		
Out of my Comfort Zone		

How I spent my time this week:

☒ Social Media

☐ Building my business

☒ Friends

☒ Working

☐

Accomplishments this week:
- Cooked all meals at home this week!!!
- Finished reading 1 book

Doodle.Doodle.Doodle.Doodle.Doodle.Doodle.Doodle.Doodle

How I will celebrate myself?
- Face mask
- Movie night
- Good food

Next Week
☐ Electric bill

☐ Doctors

☐ Groceries

☐

HAVE FUN!

Don't forget to check out the pages in the back to write notes, relax, and reset when you need it. Live your life fearlessly.

"You can, you should, and if you're brave
enough to start, you will."
Stephen King

Meal Prep Day	Meals (breakfast. lunch. dinner)

The number of hours I slept:

Zz Zz Zz Zz Zz Zz Zz Zz

Drink 70oz of water, eat healthy and exercise!

Evening Check-In

How was today great?
1. _____
2. _____

Who I look up to:

One trait to learn from them:

Important things coming up:

☐
☐
☐
☐
☐
☐

"Every morning we are born again. What we do today is what matters most."
Buddha

Date: _ _ _ _ _ _

The number of hours I slept:

Zz Zz Zz Zz Zz Zz Zz Zz

What steps will   What am I grateful for today?
I take today to   1. _____
get closer to my   2. _____
goals?

1.

2.

3.

Drink 70oz of water, eat healthy and exercise!

Evening Check-In

How would I rate my eating habits today?

1   2   3   4   5   6   7   8   9   10

Should   Win some,   Put me on
be dead   lose some   the cover of
                                       Health
                                       magazine

How many ounces of water did I drink?
1 bottle= 8 oz

How many minutes of exercise did I get today?

5   10   15   20   25   30   45   60   REST DAY

Find your joy and let it run your life

"You're more amazing than you think. I guarantee it!"
Jeff Cayley

Morning Check-In

Date: __ __ __ __

The number of hours I slept:

Zz Zz Zz Zz Zz Zz Zz Zz

What steps will
I take today to
get closer to **my**
goals?

What am I grateful for today?

1. _____
2. _____

1.
2.
3.

Drink 70oz of water, eat healthy and exercise!

Evening Check-In

How would I rate my eating habits today?

1   2   3   4   5   6   7   8   9   10

Should
be dead

Win some,
lose some

Put me on
the cover of
Health
magazine

How many ounces of water did I drink?

1 bottle = 8 oz

How many minutes of exercise did I get today?

5   10   15   20   25   30   45   60   REST DAY

Find your joy and let it run your life

"Whether you think you can, or you think you can't—you're right."
Henry Ford

Morning Check-In   Date: _ _ _ _ _ _ _

The number of hours I slept:

Zz Zz Zz Zz Zz Zz Zz Zz

What steps will   What am I grateful for today?
I take today to   1. _____
get closer to **my**   2. _____
goals?

1.   2.

                        3.

Drink 70oz of water, eat healthy and
exercise!

Evening Check-In

How would I rate my eating habits today?

1   2   3   4   5   6   7   8   9   10
Should   Win some,   Put me on
be dead   lose some   the cover of
                                       Health
                                       magazine

How many ounces of water did I drink?
1 bottle= 8 oz

How many minutes of exercise did I get today?

5   10   15   20   25   30   45   60   REST DAY

Find your joy and let it run your life

"I never dreamed about success.
I worked for it."
Estée Lauder

The number of hours I slept:

Zz Zz Zz Zz Zz Zz Zz Zz

What steps will   What am I grateful for today?
I take today to   1. _____
get closer to my   2. _____
goals?

1.   2.   3.

Drink 70oz of water, eat healthy and exercise!

Evening Check-In

How would I rate my eating habits today?

1   2   3   4   5   6   7   8   9   10

Should   Win some,   Put me on
be dead   lose some   the cover of
                                       Health
                                       magazine

How many ounces of water did I drink?
1 bottle= 8 oz

How many minutes of exercise did I get today?

5   10   15   20   25   30   45   60   REST DAY

Find your joy and let it run your life

"If you can wake up excited & go to bed proud, it's a pretty good day."
Steve Kamb

The number of hours I slept:

Zz Zz Zz Zz Zz Zz Zz Zz

What steps will I take today to get closer to **my** goals?

What am I grateful for today?

1. _____
2. _____

1.
2.
3.

Drink 70oz of water, eat healthy and exercise!

Evening Check-In

How would I rate my eating habits today?

1   2   3   4   5   6   7   8   9   10

Should be dead

Win some, lose some

Put me on the cover of Health magazine

How many ounces of water did I drink?

1 bottle= 8 oz

How many minutes of exercise did I get today?

5   10   15   20   25   30   45   60   REST DAY

Find your joy and let it run your life

"Decide that you want it more
than you are afraid of it."
Anonymous

Morning Check-In   Date: _ _ _ _ _ _

The number of hours I slept:

Zz Zz Zz Zz Zz Zz Zz Zz

What steps will   What am I grateful for today?
I take today to   1. _____
get closer to my   2. _____
goals?

1.   2.   3.

Drink 70oz of water, eat healthy and exercise!

Evening Check-In

How would I rate my eating habits today?

1   2   3   4   5   6   7   8   9   10

Should   Win some,   Put me on
be dead   lose some   the cover of
                                              Health
                                              magazine

How many ounces of water did I drink?
1 bottle= 8 oz

How many minutes of exercise did I get today?

5   10   15   20   25   30   45   60   REST DAY

Find your joy and let it run your life

Weekly Check-in

Week of ___/___

☐ Amazing   ☐ Could be better   ☐ Bad

How I spent my time this week:

How I did this week:	
Productivity	
Healthy Habits	
Out of my Comfort Zone	

Accomplishments this week:

Doodle.Doodle.Doodle.Doodle.Doodle.Doodle.Doodle.Doodle

How I will celebrate myself?

Next Week

Notepad

Notepad

"If you never want to be criticized, for goodness' sake don't do anything new."
Jeff Bezos

Meal Prep Day	Meals (breakfast, lunch, dinner)

The number of hours I slept:

Zz Zz Zz Zz Zz Zz Zz Zz

Drink 7Ooz of water, eat healthy and exercise!

Evening Check-In

How was today great?

1. _____

2. _____

Important things coming up:

Who I look up to:

One trait to learn from them:

"Nothing will work unless you do."
Maya Angelou

My Recipe for happiness:

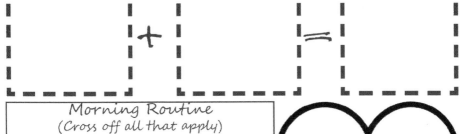

Morning Routine
(Cross off all that apply)

What I love about myself...

Drink 70oz of water, eat healthy and exercise!

Evening Check-In

How I ate today:
(draw below)

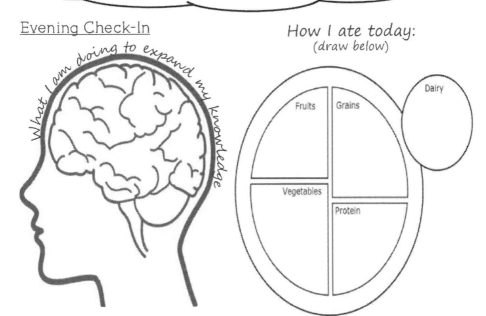

What I am doing to expand my knowledge

Find your joy and let it run your life

"The secret of getting ahead is starting. The secret of getting started is breaking your tasks into smaller manageable tasks, and then starting on the first one."
Mark Twain

My Recipe for happiness:

```
┌ ─ ─ ─ ─ ┐       ┌ ─ ─ ─ ─ ┐       ┌ ─ ─ ─ ─ ┐
            +                 =
└ ─ ─ ─ ─ ┘       └ ─ ─ ─ ─ ┘       └ ─ ─ ─ ─ ┘
```

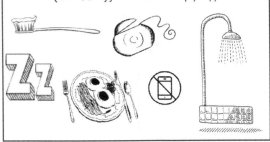

Morning Routine
(Cross off all that apply)

What I love
about myself...

Drink 70oz of water, eat healthy and exercise!

Evening Check-In

How I ate today:
(draw below)

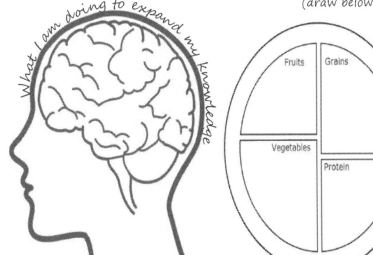

What I am doing to expand my knowledge

Dairy

Fruits   Grains

Vegetables

Protein

Find your joy and let it run your life

"Action expresses priorities."
Ghandi

Date: _ _ _ _ _ _ _

My Recipe for happiness:

[ ] + [ ] = [ ]

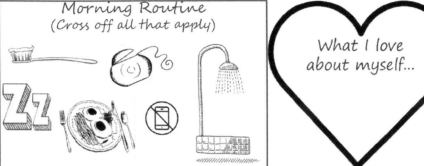

Morning Routine
(Cross off all that apply)

What I love about myself...

Drink 70oz of water, eat healthy and exercise!

Evening Check-In

What I am doing to expand my knowledge

How I ate today:
(draw below)

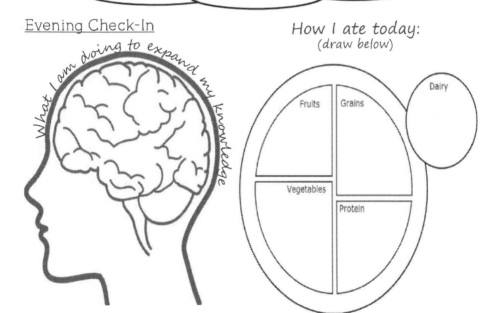

Dairy

Fruits | Grains

Vegetables

Protein

Find your joy and let it run your life

"Begin with the end in mind."
Stephen Covey

My Recipe for happiness:

Morning Routine
(Cross off all that apply)

What I love about myself...

Drink 70oz of water, eat healthy and exercise!

<u>Evening Check-In</u>

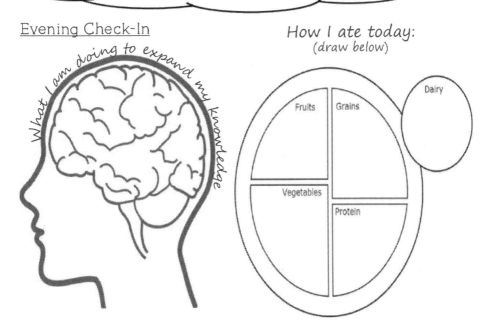

What I am doing to expand my knowledge

How I ate today:
(draw below)

Fruits   Grains   Dairy

Vegetables

Protein

Find your joy and let it run your life

"It always seems impossible until it's done."
Nelson Mandela

My Recipe for happiness:

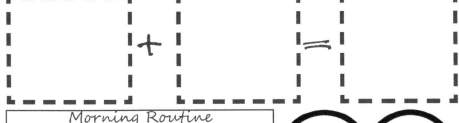

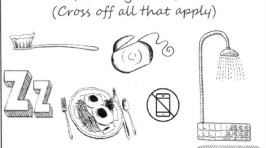

Morning Routine
(Cross off all that apply)

What I love
about myself...

Drink 70oz of water, eat healthy and
exercise!

Evening Check-In

How I ate today:
(draw below)

What I am doing to expand my knowledge

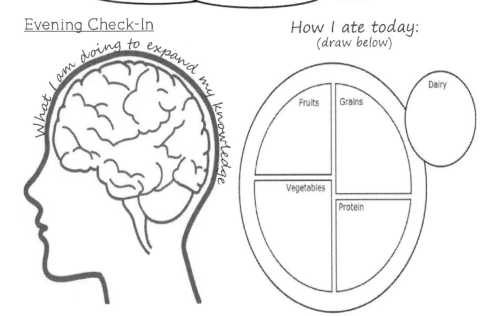

Find your joy and let it run your life

"Success is the sum of small efforts repeated day in and day out."
Robert Collier

Date: _ _ _ _ _ _

My Recipe for happiness:

```
┌ ─ ─ ─ ─ ─ ┐        ┌ ─ ─ ─ ─ ─ ┐        ┌ ─ ─ ─ ─ ─ ┐
│           │        │           │        │           │
│           │   +    │           │   =    │           │
│           │        │           │        │           │
└ ─ ─ ─ ─ ─ ┘        └ ─ ─ ─ ─ ─ ┘        └ ─ ─ ─ ─ ─ ┘
```

Morning Routine
(Cross off all that apply)

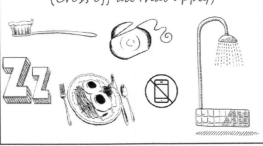

What I love about myself...

Drink 70oz of water, eat healthy and exercise!

Evening Check-In

How I ate today:
(draw below)

What I am doing to expand my knowledge

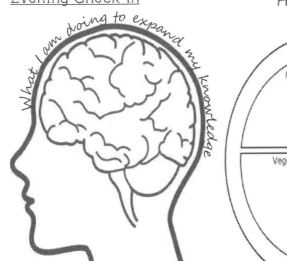

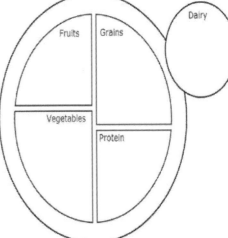

Find your joy and let it run your life

Weekly Check-in

Week of ___/___

☐ Amazing ☐ Could be better ☐ Bad

How I spent my time this week:

How I did this week:	
Productivity	
Healthy Habits	
Out of my Comfort Zone	

☐
☐
☐
☐
☐

Accomplishments this week:

Doodle. Doodle.Doodle.Doodle.Doodle.Doodle.Doodle.Doodle

How I will celebrate myself?

Next Week

☐
☐
☐
☐

Notepad

Notepad

"Imperfect action is better than perfect
inaction. Just start."
Unknown

Meal Prep Day	Meals (breakfast. lunch. dinner)

The number of hours I slept:

Zz Zz Zz Zz Zz Zz Zz Zz

Drink 7oz of water, eat healthy and exercise!

Evening Check-In

How was today great?
    1. _____
    2. _____

Who I look up to:

One trait to learn from them:

Important things coming up:

"If you just work on stuff that you like
and you're passionate about, you don't
have to have a master plan with
how things will play out."
Mark Zuckerberg

Date: _ _ _ _ _ _ _

HOW FULL IS MY glass?
(positivity in My Life)

Description of my perfect
_____:

Don't settle until I find this!

The number of hours I slept:

Zz Zz Zz Zz Zz Zz Zz Zz

Drink 70oz of water, eat healthy and exercise!

Evening Check-In

Don't sweat the small stuff.

What is bugging me?

Now let it go!

My comfort zone

Something new I tried out of my comfort zone

Find your joy and let it run your life

"Our greatest weakness lies in giving up. The most certain way to succeed is to always try one more time."
Thomas Edison

Date: _ _ _ _ _ _

HOW FULL IS MY glass?
(positivity in my life)

Description of my perfect
_____:

Don't settle until I find this!

The number of hours I slept:

Zz Zz Zz Zz Zz Zz Zz Zz

Drink 70oz of water, eat healthy and exercise!

Evening Check-In

Don't sweat the small stuff.

What is bugging me?

Now let it go!

My comfort zone

Something new I tried out of my comfort zone

Find your joy and let it run your life

"Find the smartest people you can and surround yourself with them."
Marissa Meyer

Date: _ _ _ _ _ _ _

HoW FULL iS My glass?
(poSitivity iN My LiFe)

Description of my perfect
_____:

Don't settle until I find this!

The number of hours I slept:

Zz Zz Zz Zz Zz Zz Zz Zz

Drink 70oz of water, eat healthy and exercise!

Evening Check-In

Don't sweat the small stuff.

My comfort zone

What is bugging me?

Now let it go!

Something new I tried out of my comfort zone

Find your joy and let it run your life

"Pleasure in the job, puts perfection in the work."
Aristotle

Date: _ _ _ _ _ _ _

How full is my glass?
(positivity in my life)

Description of my perfect
_____:

Don't settle until I find this!

The number of hours I slept:

Zz Zz Zz Zz Zz Zz Zz Zz Zz

Drink 70oz of water, eat healthy and exercise!

Evening Check-In

Don't sweat the small stuff.

What is bugging me?

Now let it go!

My comfort zone

Something new I tried out of my comfort zone

Find your joy and let it run your life

"Never let your small beginnings make you small-minded. Have the vision beyond your circumstances."
Brendon Burchard

Date: _ _ _ _ _ _

How FULL iS My glass?
(pOSitivity iN My LiFe)

Description of my perfect
_____:

Don't settle until I find this!

The number of hours I slept:

Zz Zz Zz Zz Zz Zz Zz Zz Zz

Drink 70oz of water, eat healthy and exercise!

Evening Check-In

Don't sweat the small stuff.

My comfort zone

What is bugging me?

Now let it go!

Something new I tried out of my comfort zone

Find your joy and let it run your life

"So often people are working hard at the wrong thing. Working on the right thing is probably more important than working hard."
Caterina Fake

Morning Check-In

HOW FULL iS MY glass?
(pOSitivity iN MY LiFe)

Description of my perfect
_____:

Don't settle until I find this!

The number of hours I slept:

Zz Zz Zz Zz Zz Zz Zz Zz Zz

Drink 70oz of water, eat healthy and exercise!

Evening Check-In

Don't sweat the small stuff.

What is bugging me?

Now let it go!

My comfort zone

Something new I tried out of my comfort zone

Find your joy and let it run your life

Weekly Check-in

Week of ___/___/___

☐ Amazing ☐ Could be better ☐ Bad

How I spent my time this week:

☐
☐
☐
☐
☐

How I did this week:	
Productivity	
Healthy Habits	
Out of my Comfort Zone	

Accomplishments this week:

Doodle. Doodle.Doodle.Doodle.Doodle.Doodle.Doodle.Doodle

How I will celebrate myself?

Next Week

☐
☐
☐
☐

Notepad

Notepad

"Your greatest self has been waiting your whole life; don't make it wait any longer."
Steve Maraboli

Date: _ _ _ _ _ _

Meal Prep Day	Meals (breakfast. lunch. dinner)

The number of hours I slept:

Zz Zz Zz Zz Zz Zz Zz Zz

Drink 70oz of water, eat healthy and exercise!

Evening Check-In

How was today great?
1. _____
2. _____

Who I look up to:

One trait to learn from them:

Important things coming up:

☐
☐
☐
☐
☐
☐

"The ones who are crazy enough to think
they can change the world,
are the ones that do."
Anonymous

Date: _ _ _ _ _ _

Morning Routine
(Cross off all that apply)

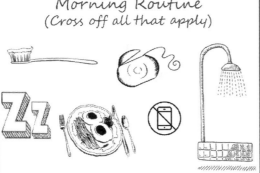

What I am learning from my reading:

My exercise plan today:

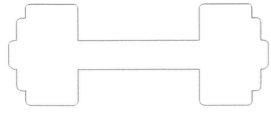

What steps I will take today to get closer to **my goals?**

1.

2.

3.

Drink 70oz of water, eat healthy and exercise!

How I balanced my life today:

Find your joy and let it run your life

"I am deliberate and afraid of nothing."
Audre Lorde

Date: _ _ _ _ _ _ _

Morning Routine
(Cross off all that apply)

What I am learning from my reading:

My exercise plan today:

What steps I will take today to get closer to **my goals?**

1.

2.

3.

Drink 70oz of water, eat healthy and exercise!

How I balanced my life today:

Find your joy and let it run your life

"Passion is energy. Feel the power
that comes from focusing on
what excites you."
Oprah Winfrey

Date: _ _ _ _ _ _

Morning Routine
(Cross off all that apply)

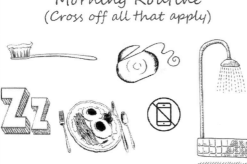

What I am learning from my reading:

My exercise plan today:

What steps I will take today to get closer to **my goals?**

1.

2.

3.

Drink 70oz of water, eat healthy and exercise!

Evening Check-In

How I balanced my life today:

Find your joy and let it run your life

"A healthy outside starts from the inside."
Robert Urich

Date: _____

Morning Routine
(Cross off all that apply)

What I am learning
from my reading:

My exercise plan today:

What steps I will take today to get closer to **my goals?**

1.
2.
3.

Drink 70oz of water, eat healthy and exercise!

Evening Check-In

How I balanced my life today:

Find your joy and let it run your life

"When you are content to be simply yourself and don't compare or compete, everyone will respect you."
Lao Tzu

Date: _ _ _ _ _ _ _

Morning Routine
(Cross off all that apply)

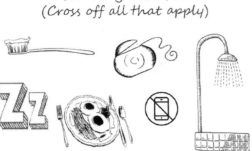

What I am learning from my reading:

My exercise plan today:

What steps I will take today to get closer to **my goals**?

1.

2.

3.

Drink 70oz of water, eat healthy and exercise!

How I balanced my life today:

Find your joy and let it run your life

"Do one thing every day that scares you."
Anonymous

<u>Morning Check-In</u>

Date: _ _ _ _ _ _ _

Morning Routine
(Cross off all that apply)

What I am learning
from my reading:

My exercise plan today:

What steps I will take today to get closer to **my goals?**

1.

2.

3.

Drink 70oz of water, eat healthy and exercise!

<u>Evening Check-In</u>

How I balanced my life today:

Find your joy and let it run your life

Weekly Check-in

You are getting close to the end of this journal, don't forget to order your new journal!

Don't quit now! You are impressing everyone!

Week of ___/___

☐ Amazing ☐ Could be better ☐ Bad

How I spent my time this week:

How I did this week:	
Productivity	
Healthy Habits	
Out of my Comfort Zone	

☐
☐
☐
☐
☐

Accomplishments this week:

Doodle. Doodle. Doodle. Doodle. Doodle. Doodle. Doodle. Doodle

How I will celebrate myself?

Next Week

☐
☐
☐
☐

Notepad

Notepad

"If people are not laughing at your goals,
your goals are too small."
Azim Premji

Meal Prep Day	Meals (breakfast. lunch. dinner)

The number of hours I slept:

Zz Zz Zz Zz Zz Zz Zz Zz

Drink 70oz of water, eat healthy and exercise!

Evening Check-In

How was today great?

1. _____

2. _____

Who I look up to:

One trait to learn from them:

Important things coming up:

☐
☐
☐
☐
☐
☐

"When it is obvious that the goals cannot be reached, don't adjust the goals, adjust the action steps."
Confucius

Morning Check-In   Date: _ _ _ _ _ _

What I love
about myself...

My exercise plan today:

How I will pay it forward

The number of hours I slept:

ZzZzZzZzZzZzZzZzZzZzZz

Drink 70oz of water, eat healthy and
exercise!

Evening Check-In

Spend 5 minutes
thinking BIG
(Write or draw your thoughts)

What made me happy
today?

Find your joy and let it run your life

"I cannot give you the formula for success,
but I can give you the formula for failure,
which is: Try to please everybody."
Herbert Swope

Date: _ _ _ _ _ _

My exercise plan today:

What I love
about myself...

How I will pay it forward

The number of hours I slept:

ZzZzZzZzZzZzZzZzZzZz

Drink 70oz of water, eat healthy and
exercise!

Evening Check-In

What made me happy
today?

Spend 5 minutes
thinking BIG
(Write or draw your thoughts)

Find your joy and let it run your life

"Do you want to know who you are?
Don't ask. Act! Action will delineate and
define you."
Thomas Jefferson

Morning Check-In

Date: _ _ _ _ _ _

My exercise plan today:

What I love about myself...

How I will pay it forward

The number of hours I slept:

ZzZzZzZzZzZzZzZzZzZz

Drink 7oz of water, eat healthy and exercise!

Evening Check-In

What made me happy today?

Spend 5 minutes thinking BIG
(Write or draw your thoughts)

Find your joy and let it run your life

"What are you waiting for?"
Ilore De Vegas

Date: _ _ _ _ _ _

My exercise plan today:

What I love about myself...

How I will pay it forward

The number of hours I slept:

ZzZzZzZzZzZzZzZzZzZz

Drink 70oz of water, eat healthy and exercise!

Evening Check-In

What made me happy today?

Spend 5 minutes thinking BIG
(Write or draw your thoughts)

Find your joy and let it run your life

"I know society says you should be a certain way, but I think [you should] stop and look at what is your natural way of being who you are."
Ari Horie

Morning Check-In

Date: _ _ _ _ _ _

My exercise plan today:

What I love about myself...

How I will pay it forward

The number of hours I slept:

ZzZzZzZz ZzZzZzZz ZzZzZzZz

Drink 70oz of water, eat healthy and exercise!

Evening Check-In

What made me happy today?

Spend 5 minutes thinking BIG
(Write or draw your thoughts)

Find your joy and let it run your life

"So many of our dreams at first seem impossible, then they seem improbable, and then, when we summon the will, they soon become inevitable."
Christopher Reeve

Date: _ _ _ _ _ _

My exercise plan today:

What I love about myself...

How I will pay it forward

The number of hours I slept:

ZzZzZzZzZzZzZzZzZzZz

Drink 70oz of water, eat healthy and exercise!

Evening Check-In

What made me happy today?

Spend 5 minutes thinking BIG
(Write or draw your thoughts)

Find your joy and let it run your life

Weekly Check-in

Week of __ __ / __ __

☐ Amazing ☐ Could be better ☐ Bad

How I did this week:

Productivity	
Healthy Habits	
Out of my Comfort Zone	

How I spent my time this week:

☐
☐
☐
☐
☐

Accomplishments this week:

Doodle. Doodle. Doodle. Doodle. Doodle. Doodle. Doodle. Doodle

How I will celebrate myself?

Next Week

☐
☐
☐
☐

Notepad

Notepad

If you wish to move mountains
tomorrow, you must start by
lifting small stones today.
African Proverb

What is your quote? (Create a legacy here)

Meal Prep Day	Meals (breakfast. lunch. dinner)

The number of hours I slept:

Zz Zz Zz Zz Zz Zz Zz Zz

Drink 70oz of water, eat healthy and exercise!

Evening Check-In

How was today great?

1. _____

2. _____

Who I look up to:

One trait to learn from them:

Important things coming up:

"If you want something you've never had,
you must be willing to do
something you've never done."
Thomas Jefferson

Issues in my life today: How I can overcome them:

➡️

My Recipe for happiness today:

⌐ ¬   ⌐ ¬   ⌐ ¬
¦   ¦ + ¦   ¦ = ¦   ¦
⌐ ¬   ⌐ ¬   ⌐ ¬

Drink 70oz of water, eat healthy and exercise!

How would I rate my eating habits today?

1   2   3   4   5   6   7   8   9   10

Should
be dead

Win some,
lose some

Put me on
the cover of
Health
magazine

How many ounces of water did I drink?
1 bottle= 8 oz

How many minutes of exercise did I get today?

5   10   15   20   25   30   45   60   REST DAY

Find your joy and let it run your life

"Chase the vision, not the money; the money will end up following you."
Tony Hsieh

<u>Morning Check-In</u>   Date: _ _ _ _ _ _

Issues in my life today: How I can overcome them:

➡️

My Recipe for happiness today:

[ ] + [ ] = [ ]

Drink 70oz of water, eat healthy and exercise!

<u>Evening Check-In</u>

How would I rate my eating habits today?

1   2   3   4   5   6   7   8   9   10

Should   Win some,   Put me on
be dead   lose some   the cover of
                                       Health
                                       magazine

How many ounces of water did I drink?
1 bottle= 8 oz

How many minutes of exercise did I get today?

5   10   15   20   25   30   45   60   REST DAY

Find your joy and let it run your life

"If your actions inspire others to dream more, learn more, do more and become more, you are a leader."
John Quincy Adams

<u>Morning Check-In</u>   Date: _ _ _ _ _ _

Issues in my life today: How I can overcome them:

➡️

My Recipe for happiness today:

[ ] + [ ] = [ ]

Drink 70oz of water, eat healthy and exercise!

<u>Evening Check-In</u>

How would I rate my eating habits today?

1   2   3   4   5   6   7   8   9   10
Should   Win some,   Put me on
be dead   lose some   the cover of
                                       Health
                                       magazine

How many ounces of water did I drink?
1 bottle= 8 oz

How many minutes of exercise did I get today?

5   10   15   20   25   30   45   60   REST DAY

Find your joy and let it run your life

"Start where you are.
Use what you have.
Do what you can."
Arthur Ashe

<u>Morning Check-In</u>   Date: _ _ _ _ _ _

Issues in my life today: How I can overcome them:

➡️

My Recipe for happiness today:

⌐ ⌐ ⌐ ¬   +   ⌐ ⌐ ⌐ ¬   =   ⌐ ⌐ ⌐ ¬

Drink 70oz of water, eat healthy and exercise!

<u>Evening Check-In</u>

How would I rate my eating habits today?

1   2   3   4   5   6   7   8   9   10

Should   Win some,   Put me on
be dead   lose some   the cover of
                                      Health
                                      magazine

How many ounces of water did I drink?
1 bottle= 8 oz

How many minutes of exercise did I get today?

5   10   15   20   25   30   45   60   REST DAY

Find your joy and let it run your life

"The mind, once stretched by a new idea, never regains its original dimensions."
Oliver Wendell Holmes

<u>Morning Check-In</u>   Date: _ _ _ _ _ _

Issues in my life today:	How I can overcome them:

My Recipe for happiness today:

Drink 70oz of water, eat healthy and exercise!

<u>Evening Check-In</u>

How would I rate my eating habits today?

1   2   3   4   5   6   7   8   9   10

Should
be dead

Win some,
lose some

Put me on
the cover of
Health
magazine

How many ounces of water did I drink?

1 bottle= 8 oz

How many minutes of exercise did I get today?

5   10   15   20   25   30   45   60   REST DAY

Find your joy and let it run your life

"The path to success is to take massive determined action."
Tony Robbins

Issues in my life today: How I can overcome them:

➡️

My Recipe for happiness today:

⌐ ⌐ ⌐ ⌐ ⌐   ⌐ ⌐ ⌐ ⌐ ⌐   ⌐ ⌐ ⌐ ⌐ ⌐

+   =

Drink 70oz of water, eat healthy and exercise!

How would I rate my eating habits today?

1   2   3   4   5   6   7   8   9   10

Should   Win some,   Put me on
be dead   lose some   the cover of
                                           Health
                                           magazine

How many ounces of water did I drink?

1 bottle= 8 oz

How many minutes of exercise did I get today?

5   10   15   20   25   30   45   60   REST DAY

Find your joy and let it run your life

Weekly Check-in

Week of _ _ / _ _

- [ ] Amazing
- [ ] Could be better
- [ ] Bad

How I spent my time this week:

- [ ]
- [ ]
- [ ]
- [ ]
- [ ]

How I did this week:	
Productivity	
Healthy Habits	
Out of my Comfort Zone	

Accomplishments this week:

Doodle. Doodle. Doodle. Doodle. Doodle. Doodle. Doodle. Doodle

How I will celebrate myself?

Next Week

- [ ]
- [ ]
- [ ]
- [ ]

Notepad

Notepad

"You often feel tired, not because you've done too much, but because you've done too little of what sparks a light in you."
Unknown

Meal Prep Day	Meals (breakfast. lunch. dinner)

The number of hours I slept:

Zz Zz Zz Zz Zz Zz Zz Zz

Drink 70oz of water, eat healthy and exercise!

Evening Check-In

How was today great?
1. _____
2. _____

Who I look up to:

One trait to learn from them:

Important things coming up:

☐
☐
☐
☐
☐
☐

"Be thankful for what you have; you'll end up having more. If you concentrate on what you don't have,
you will never, ever have enough."
Oprah Winfrey

<u>Morning Check-In</u>   Date: _ _ _ _ _ _

The number of hours I slept:

Zz Zz Zz Zz Zz Zz Zz Zz

What steps will   What am I grateful for today?
I take today to   1. _____
get closer to my 2. _____
goals?

1.
2.
3.

Drink 70oz of water, eat healthy and exercise!

<u>Evening Check-In</u>

How would I rate my eating habits today?

1   2   3   4   5   6   7   8   9   10
Should   Win some,   Put me on
be dead   lose some   the cover of
                                         Health
                                         magazine

How many ounces of water did I drink?
1 bottle= 8 oz

How many minutes of exercise did I get today?

5   10   15   20   25   30   45   60   REST DAY

Find your joy and let it run your life

"Growth is painful. Change is painful.
But nothing is as painful as staying stuck
somewhere you don't belong."
Mandy Hale

My Recipe for happiness:

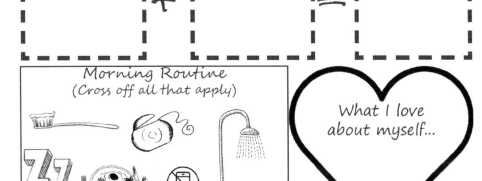

[dashed box]   +   [dashed box]   =   [dashed box]

Morning Routine
(Cross off all that apply)

What I love about myself...

Drink 7Ooz of water, eat healthy and exercise!

How I ate today:
(draw below)

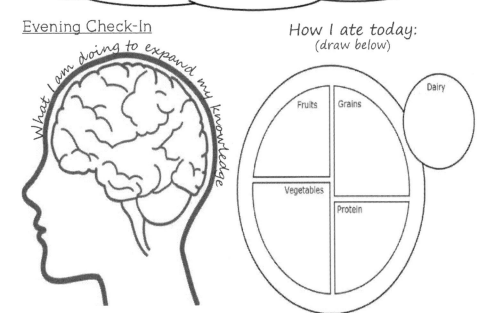

What I am doing to expand my knowledge

Fruits   Grains

Dairy

Vegetables

Protein

Find your joy and let it run your life

"Don't give up trying to do what you really want to do."
Ella Fitzgerald

HOW FULL IS MY glass?
(positivity in My LiFe)

Description of my perfect
_____:

Don't settle until I find this!

The number of hours I slept:

Zz Zz Zz Zz Zz Zz Zz Zz

Drink 70oz of water, eat healthy and exercise!

Evening Check-In

Don't sweat the small stuff.

What is bugging me?

Now let it go!

My comfort zone

Something new I tried out of my comfort zone

Find your joy and let it run your life

"When something is important enough,
you do it even if the odds are
not in your favor."
Elon Musk

<u>Morning Check-In</u>

Date: _ _ _ _ _ _ _

Morning Routine
(Cross off all that apply)

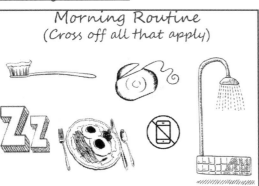

What I am learning from my reading:

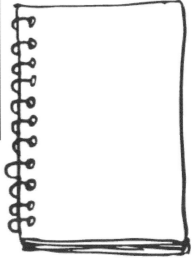

My exercise plan today:

What steps I will take today to get closer to **my goals?**

1.

2.

3.

Drink 70oz of water, eat healthy and exercise!

<u>Evening Check-In</u>

How I balanced my life today:

Find your joy and let it run your life

"Fall in love with the process and
the results will follow."
Bradley Whitford

<u>Morning Check-In</u>   Date: _ _ _ _ _ _

Issues in my life today: How I can overcome them:

➡️

My Recipe for happiness today:

[ ] + [ ] = [ ]

Drink 70oz of water, eat healthy and exercise!

<u>Evening Check-In</u>

How would I rate my eating habits today?

1   2   3   4   5   6   7   8   9   10

Should   Win some,   Put me on
be dead   lose some   the cover of
                                     Health
                                     magazine

How many ounces of water did I drink?
1 bottle= 8 oz

How many minutes of exercise did I get today?

5   10   15   20   25   30   45   60   REST DAY

Find your joy and let it run your life

"Give yourself permission to slow down.
You can speed up by slowing down."
Gabby Bernstein

Morning Check-In   Date: _ _ _ _ _ _

My exercise plan today:

What I love about myself...

How I will pay it forward

The number of hours I slept:

ZzZzZzZzZzZzZzZzZz

Drink 70oz of water, eat healthy and exercise!

Evening Check-In

What made me happy today?

Spend 5 minutes thinking BIG
(Write or draw your thoughts)

Find your joy and let it run your life

Weekly Check-in

You killed it in this journal! We are so proud of you! Share your success with us by tagging #neverstaystagnant

Keep up your wonderful life! The next few pages are filled with activities to help you relax and reset.

Week of ___/___/___

☐ Amazing ☐ Could be better ☐ Bad

How I spent my time this week:

How I did this week:	
Productivity	
Healthy Habits	
Out of my Comfort Zone	

☐
☐
☐
☐
☐

Accomplishments this week:

Doodle. Doodle. Doodle. Doodle. Doodle. Doodle. Doodle. Doodle

How I will celebrate myself?

Next Week

☐
☐
☐
☐

Notepad

Notepad

Notepad

Notepad

Notepad

Notepad

Drawing Space

Drawing Space

life is better

with a smile

Made in the USA
Las Vegas, NV
05 February 2021